HISPANIC STAR

CELIA CRUZ

THE HISPANIC STAR SERIES

Read about the most groundbreaking, iconic Hispanic heroes who have shaped our culture and the world in this gripping biography series for young readers.

IF YOU CAN SEE IT, YOU CAN BE IT.

CELIA CRUZ

CLAUDIA ROMO EDELMAN
AND **WILLIAM ALEXANDER**

ILLUSTRATED BY **ALEXANDRA BEGUEZ**

ROARING BROOK PRESS

NEW YORK

Published by Roaring Brook Press
Roaring Brook Press is a division of Holtzbrinck Publishing Holdings Limited
Partnership
120 Broadway, New York, NY 10271 • mackids.com

Our books may be purchased in bulk for promotional, educational, or business
use. Please contact your local bookseller or the Macmillan Corporate and
Premium Sales Department at (800) 221-7945 ext. 5442 or by email at
MacmillanSpecialMarkets@macmillan.com.

Library of Congress Cataloging-in-Publication Data

Names: Romo Edelman, Claudia, author. | Alexander, William (William Joseph),
    1976– author. | Beguez, Alexandra, illustrator.
Title: Celia Cruz / Claudia Romo Edelman and William Alexander ; illustrations
    by Alexandra Beguez.
Description: New York : Roaring Brook Press, 2022. | Series: Hispanic star |
    Audience: Ages 7–9 | Audience: Grades 2–3 | Summary: "Meet the Queen of Salsa,
    Celia Cruz—once just a girl from Havana, Cuba, who loved to sing. Her soulful
    voice, compelling charm, and unstoppable determination led to her meteoric rise
    to fame, opening the door for Latinx performers everywhere. Her booming
    career took her from the Sonora Matancera to the Fania All-Stars, with the rising
    popularity of salsa, a genre born of Afro-Cuban musical stylings. Six decades
    and more than seventy albums later, Celia's influence still has an undeniable
    hold on today's music"— Provided by publisher.
Identifiers: LCCN 2022027150 | ISBN 9781250828125 (hardback) |
    ISBN 9781250828132 (trade paperback)
Subjects: LCSH: Cruz, Celia—Juvenile literature. | Singers—Latin America—
    Biography—Juvenile literature. | Women singers—Latin America—Biography—
    Juvenile literature. | Salsa musicians—Latin America—Biography—Juvenile
    literature.
Classification: LCC ML3930.C96 R66 2022 | DDC 782.42164092 [B]—
    dc23/eng/20220610
LC record available at https://lccn.loc.gov/2022027150

First edition, 2022
Book design by Samira Iravani
Printed in the United States of America by Lakeside Book Company, Crawfordsville,
Indiana

ISBN 978-1-250-82813-2 (paperback)
10 9 8 7 6 5 4 3 2 1

ISBN 978-1-250-82812-5 (hardcover)
10 9 8 7 6 5 4 3 2 1

For my mom, who lost her battle to Covid, but whose values live in me every day. I am who I am because she was the best of role models.

For my husband, Richard, and children, Joshua and Tamara, who surround me with their love, their belief in me, and support. They make it all possible.

Most of all, this series is dedicated to the children of tomorrow. We know that you have to see it to be it. We hope these Latino heroes teach you to spread your wings and fly.
—C. R. E.

Para mi padre.
—W. A.

CHAPTER ONE

THE GIRL WHO CARVED HER NAME IN THE AIR

Celia's home was both happy and crowded. Her parents, three siblings, one grandmother, a few aunts, and a whole bunch of cousins squeezed into their small first-floor tenement with two bedrooms and a single bathroom. As many as fourteen kids lived at 47 Serrano Street when Celia was young, and it was her job to sing lullabies at bedtime to everyone younger than she was. This backfired

every time. Celia could not sing the smaller kids to sleep. They refused to sleep. All of them stayed awake and demanded endless encores of every lullaby.

Protective metal bars covered the first-floor windows in Santos Suárez, a working-class neighborhood in southern Havana. Those bars tried to look intimidating, but the Cruz family home did not lock itself away from the rest of the city. Their front door was always propped wide open to welcome conversations with neighbors and the cooling Caribbean breeze.

If you walked by their open door in the afternoon, you would probably hear Celia's mother singing to herself in the kitchen. You would also smell her cooking: white rice and black beans on an ordinary day, sizzling slices of plátanos and the slow simmer of ropa vieja on special occasions.

Celia would always remember that meal as her unsurpassed favorite, and the smell of it simmering on the stove—which took all afternoon—conjured memories of her mother's singing voice.

ROPA VIEJA means "old clothes" in Spanish. If cooked properly, the shredded beef falls apart like threadbare clothing.

If you walked along Serrano Street in the evening, you would hear Celia herself singing lullabies to the household's younger kids. Her voice would carry through the bars outside their shared bedroom window. It would carry through the open front door. Neighbors would gather to listen. You would gather with them, becoming a part of that sudden, unplanned audience. It wouldn't matter where you thought you were going at the time. If you could hear Celia sing, then you had no reason to be anywhere else.

Sometimes she paused, went outside, and told the crowd of neighbors to please go away. They always came back.

As a young girl in south Havana, Celia never guessed that she would one day become Cuba's cultural ambassador to the rest of the world, praised as the greatest voice in a generation.

Úrsula Hilaria Celia Caridad Cruz Alfonso was born on October 21, 1925, at 47 Serrano Street in Havana—the capital city of the Caribbean nation of Cuba, approximately one hundred miles south from the Florida Keys.

Her parents named her Úrsula because she was born on the feast day of Saint Úrsula, patron of schoolgirls, but her mother insisted on calling her Celia instead. Saint Celia is the patron of music, and music was vital to that side of the family. Her mom—known to everyone by her nickname Ollita—was always singing. Celia later insisted that her mother's voice lifted in song was the first sound that she heard while still in the womb. The calming timbre of that voice continued to be an ever-present soundtrack throughout her childhood.

For her part, Ollita was so proud of her daughter's voice that she took every opportunity to show her off. Celia sang for family guests when she was still too young to feel self-conscious about doing so. After one performance of "¿Y tú qué has hecho?"—a folk song about a girl who carves her name into the bark of a tree—the guests were so impressed that they bought Celia a new pair of white leather shoes.

One of the neighbors on Serrano Street provided back-yard lessons in Caribbean musical history by way of Lucumi songs and ceremonies—a syncretic combination of European Catholicism from Spain and African religious traditions of the Yoruba people. These traditions had survived the atrocities of the Middle Passage, blended with Catholicism during centuries of slavery, and continued to thrive in contemporary Havana. Celia's mother was afraid of Lucumi, and called it Santería. Celia's brother, Bárbaro, would one

day become a santero himself and use the family gift for
music to sing Lucumi songs of devotion. Celia herself sat
under a ceiba tree in the corner of her backyard and listened close whenever their santera neighbor hosted bembé
drum celebrations. Years later, Celia would find inspira-
tion, ancestry, and solace in Afro-Cuban music of diaspora.

As an older kid, Celia went dancing with her friends
and cousins at the Sociedad de los Jóvenes del Vals—a
neighborhood social club on Rodriguez Street—where
she heard live performances by legendary musicians. She

would sit as close to the stage as possible whenever her favorite singer, Paulina Álvarez, performed to the beat of her handheld wooden claves.

Celia was fourteen when she snuck out to see the Havana carnaval for the very first time. She felt thrilled, terrified, and horribly guilty about lying to her mother and pretending to spend the whole day at her friend Caridad's place. (Meanwhile, Caridad's parents thought that their daughter was over at Celia's.) Celia also felt physically uncomfortable on the bus, because she had to sit on her cousin Nenita's lap for the entire ride. Bus fare was just a nickel in 1940, but there were six of them, and they only had enough pocket change for five tickets, so Celia and Nenita needed to share a seat.

They took the bus from Santos Suárez to central Havana, crossing the length of a city so beautiful, powerful, and coveted by the colonial powers of Europe that when British pirates occupied Havana in 1762, Spain traded the whole peninsula of Florida to get it back. England could not maintain their new claim on Florida for very long, though; the mainland colonies that would become the United States defeated the British at Yorktown in 1781.

Cuba wrested independence from Spain a century later. Celia's maternal grandfather fought as a mambí for that freedom. Soon afterward the island nation of Cuba restored its centuries-old traditions of carnaval: a multiday hurricane of music, dancing, parades, and processions in resplendent clothes and costumes.

Carnaval in Havana was like nothing else in the world. Fourteen-year-old Celia Cruz had never seen it, though, despite living in the city for her entire life. Celia's mother and father had never let her go. Her parents had no idea that their daughter had snuck out to hear the rhythms of bembé and watch costumed processions of dancers overwhelm Havana.

A fierce joy woke in Celia on that day of carnaval, and for the rest of her days it would never leave her.

The six friends had a long walk home to Santos Suárez afterward. None of them had any money left for the bus ride back.

Celia snuck home without getting caught, exhausted but still unable to sleep. The excitement and adrenaline of carnaval kept her awake. So did the guilt. She hated lying, to anyone, for any reason whatsoever, and she hated lying to Ollita most of all.

The next morning, Celia quietly confessed to Tía Ana, her mother's sister.

Ana gently scolded her niece for sneaking out. Then she asked if Celia wanted to go back.

The two co-conspirators returned to carnaval that afternoon. Tía Ana made excuses about needing help with errands, which spared Celia's conscience the burden of lying to Ollita two days in a row.

Auntie and niece arrived at the capitol building, the very center of the joyous storm. They sang and danced alongside the costumed troupes of comparsas until the two of them couldn't feel their feet anymore. By the time they returned home, very late at night, Celia's father was already asleep. Her mother, clearly undeceived by their sneaky cover story, stayed awake to welcome them back with conspiratorial hugs.

That night, Celia dreamed she was the Queen of Carnaval. She wore a long white gown and held her arms wide to the world as she sang.

In 1944, just a couple of weeks before Celia's nineteenth birthday, a devastating hurricane passed through Havana. Storm winds humbled royal palm trees and sent them flying. Celia was sure that their home on Serrano Street would collapse over their heads, but the walls held strong.

Another young musician was badly shaken by that same storm. Pedro Knight, a tall trumpet player, worked for a traveling circus that year. Hurricane winds were unkind to the circus tents. Afterward, as Havana slowly pulled itself back together, no one had any spare cash to spend on a damaged circus. Unfed, unpaid performers ate little more than bread crusts in the lean weeks that followed.

Celia's heart would have broken for them if she had known, but Celia had yet to meet the tall trumpet player Pedro Knight.

Young Celia Cruz intended to become a teacher when she grew up. That was the plan she inherited from her serious, hardworking, and practical-minded father. Celia liked school, loved kids, and shared a first name with the patron saint of schoolgirls. It seemed perfectly natural for her career to lead back to a classroom of her own.

A crossroads moment arrived in 1947, when two wildly

different versions of Celia's life stretched out in front of her. She was already enrolled in the Escuela Normal de Maestros for teacher training when her cousin Serafín secretly signed her up for a singing contest at a local radio station.

Celia felt overjoyed, nervous with stage fright, grateful to her cousin, and annoyed with him for signing her name without asking her first. Serafín made no apologies, though. He knew what music meant to Celia. He also knew what Celia's voice meant to everyone else.

The contest was held on a Saturday. Celia woke up extra early that morning. She felt confident, her former nervousness gone. She wore a white dress, and her mother styled her hair into a tight bun behind her head. In the mirror she looked exactly like her dream of the Queen of Carnaval. Outside, early-morning sunlight sparkled on dewdrops like sequins under stage lights.

Serafín went with Celia to the radio station. It was only twelve blocks from the house, and they were used to walking everywhere, but on that day the two of them rode the bus instead. Most of the other contestants at the station were older than Celia, which made her feel a bit naive and out of place. Then she took her turn at the microphone and sang "Nostalgia," a tango accompanied by the beat of handheld wooden claves. She had brought them in honor of Paulina Álvarez, her favorite singer, and now they unlocked her voice.

Celia won first place.

Her prize was a cake from La Casa Potín, one of the best and fanciest bakeries in Havana. Celia and Serafín brought the cake home in triumph—he was even more excited about her musical victory than she was—and shared that sugary feast with the whole family. Celia would always remember the deliciously delicate taste of that cake.

She won a necklace when she took first place in the

next contest, and after that she signed up for every singing competition she could find. Serafín continued to help as her unofficial agent. The two of them brought home prize after prize—sometimes money, sometimes chocolate, and sometimes household necessities like condensed milk, bread, and soap. Every new victory sparked a party at home, where *almost* every family member laughed, talked, and sang over one another.

Celia's father was the only one who refused to celebrate her victories. He radiated cold, quiet displeasure whenever his daughter made a public display of her voice.

Simón Cruz worked the railroads.

He shoveled coal all day.

He never sang.

Whenever the topic of Celia's future came up in conversation, her father continued to insist that she would become a teacher. Celia didn't argue. She kept up with her classes, learned more about literature and the art of teaching, and paid for her textbooks with the money that she kept winning from radio contests.

Her mother told her not to worry too much about her father's coldness. Celia did worry, though. She keenly felt the lack of his respect. Ollita and Tía Ana offered extra helpings of warmth and support to compensate.

One day Ana joined her niece to watch her perform in yet another radio contest. Celia won—as usual—but the win clearly belonged to her voice alone and not to her presence onstage. Afterward Ana gently pointed out that Celia had stood like a statue. She didn't dance. She barely even moved. She seemed immune to the power of her own voice. Tía Ana told her that an audience couldn't feel the emotion, rhythm, or momentum of music unless the musician allowed herself to be moved by it first. That wasn't something Celia wanted to hear. It took a little of the shine away from her latest vocal victory. She still appreciated her tía's critique, though, and she understood why she held very still at the microphone: Celia was afraid. Some part of her held back, reluctant to accept and command the focused attention of stage and spotlight. She was a gifted singer, and she knew that—*everyone* knew that— but Celia was not yet a performer.

She vowed to become one.

After Tía Ana told her to unfreeze at the microphone, Celia took every opportunity she could find to perform in front of a live audience. She sang at parties and neighborhood events with the local band El Botón de Oro—the Golden Button, named for the gold flower-shaped buttons they wore. She sang accompaniment to every show and ceremony at the teachers' college. She sang on graduation day in 1949—a day that would turn out to be another crossroads moment.

After the commencement ceremony ended, Celia found herself in conversation with Marta Rainieri, one of her favorite teachers at the college. Celia asked for advice about becoming a teacher herself. Ms. Rainieri gave her a stern look, spoke with a serious tone, and told Celia that she had more of a gift for singing onstage than lecturing in the classroom. She urged Celia to honor that gift. (Ms. Rainieri also confessed that teachers' salaries were much too small.)

Celia felt surprised and thrilled to be seen, heard, and recognized for who she really was.

Savor that moment along with her. Think about a time when you felt seen and understood by a teacher. (Hopefully you have at least one such moment to remember.) Enjoy the irony that Ms. Rainieri demonstrated the life-changing power of a good teacher by telling Celia not to become one and to follow her musical calling instead.

This was the moment when Celia stopped trying to simultaneously embrace two different versions of her future: the one she wanted for herself, and the one her father wanted for her. She set teaching aside and set out to conquer the music business instead.

Simón Cruz withdrew further into his shell of cold, quiet anger.

Celia ignored him as much as she could.

Her conquest began at Havana's Academia Municipal de Música; Celia may have buried her former plans to become a teacher, but she continued to feed her curiosity and intellect by studying musical theory at the academy. There, she continued to train her rare contralto voice, which is the lowest gendered range for female singers. A male voice hitting the same notes is called a tenor.

Celia also found private tutors for piano lessons, with mixed success. She couldn't stand her first piano teacher, for reasons that Celia herself never fully understood; the two of them just clashed. She learned more from Oscar

Muñoz Boufartique, who urged Celia to cut her long finger-nails in order to better play the piano keys. She absolutely refused. Celia later joked about it and said that she regretted missing the chance to become a better pianist when she was young. She could have grown the nails back afterward.

The rest of Celia's training took place on the job, in radio studios throughout Havana—especially CMQ radio station in El Vedado, a neighborhood just south of the Malecón.

THE MALECÓN is a road and seawall that does its best to keep Caribbean waves out of Havana, and mostly succeeds.

Freelance musicians and actors showed up in the morning; checked a notebook to see if they were on call for any of the rehearsals, shows, or commercial jingles scheduled for the day; and then sat on a bench in the reception office to wait. They called it "the bench of dreams," a place for daydreaming about future stardom.

That bench was also a place of careful study. Celia spent many long hours observing the other performers: how they conducted themselves in rehearsal, which techniques they used to warm up before a show, and—most important—the way that they treated one another. This was a community rather than a random collection of freelancers in cutthroat competition. Musicians supported one another, looked out for one another, and offered guidance and advice to newcomers like Celia on the bench of dreams.

All of them needed that support and camaraderie, because all radio was *live* radio in the 1940s. Every word, note, and accidental noise hit the airwaves immediately. Every script and song needed to be memorized. Every mistake meant that you might not get hired for the next show, and *everyone* made mistakes. Celia learned how to take the work seriously, and how to joke about the inevitable mishaps in order to stay confident and keep from panicking the next time. She learned how to roll with the uncontrollable nature of live performance and just keep going, no matter what happened, because there was never any turning back for a second take.

Celia developed skills to match her talent at the microphones of the CMQ radio studios. She also gained the love and respect of her new musical community.

Meanwhile, the love and respect of Celia's father seemed impossible to earn. The two of them barely spoke. He strongly believed that show business was a humiliating, degenerate life for any woman to undertake—and that his daughter brought contagious shame down on the whole family every time she performed.

The man clung to his stubborn beliefs for years, barely acknowledging that Celia even existed until the day that a railway coworker showed him a newspaper article about a rising radio star.

At first Simón was mortified. Then he actually read the article. He paid close attention to every word of praise for Celia's talent and skill. He glimpsed the star performer that the whole city of Havana had begun to adore and for the first time saw his daughter truly.

That night, after a long workday of shoveling coal, Simón Cruz sat down with Celia for their first proper conversation in years. He tried to explain why he had felt so ashamed before and why he would never deny her again. He told Celia that he trusted her.

To everyone reading these pages: May you also be seen, heard, and understood.

CHAPTER TWO

NEVER BOW YOUR HEAD TO ANYONE

The love and support of Celia's family remained the bedrock foundation of her professional success as a singer and radio star. She had always been close to her cousins—especially Nenita and Serafín—and it was Nenita who switched on the family radio and insisted that Celia listen to the Sonora Matancera orchestra.

This legendary ensemble of Afro-Cuban musicians was first founded in 1924 in Matanzas, a province of Cuba just east of Havana and "the forging furnace of Cuban music," according to musicologist Helio Orovio.

The band moved to Havana in 1927 (when Celia was two years old), cut their first albums in 1928 when she was three, then signed with Radio Progreso to perform a regular series of live shows. Twenty years later, Nenita tuned the radio dial to that same show.

Celia listened, entranced.

That night she could barely sleep. The Sonora Matancera continued to play in her mind and memory. When sleep finally came, Celia dreamed herself into another white gown. She stood center stage at Havana's great Campoamor Theater, and the Sonora Matancera played behind her as she sang.

By the year 1950 Celia was becoming an increasingly big deal. She recorded her first albums with a few different bands (though one of them neglected to pay her for the work), and she continued to line up regular gigs at Radio Cadena Suaritos (which didn't pay very well, either). Show business was a struggle and a hustle, as always, but Celia managed to make it work.

Her dream of singing with the Sonora Matancera was unlikely to ever happen. That band was like a superhero team, both in their popularity and in the fact that they only ever included one woman in their ranks. The Justice League has Wonder Woman, the Avengers begins with either Black Widow (in the movies) or the Wasp (in the comics), and the Sonora Matancera already boasted the great Puerto Rican performer Myrta Silva as their lead singer.

Celia set her dream aside and tried not to think about it. Then a mysterious gentleman named Sotolongo stopped by the studios at Radio Cadena Suaritos and asked to speak with her. (She never learned his first name. As far as she knew the man only ever went by "Mr. Sotolongo," which makes this moment seem like something out of a spy movie.) Mr. Sotolongo gave Celia the secret news that Myrta Silva intended to return home to Puerto Rico. The great

Built a century ago, in 1921, the CAMPOAMOR was modeled after the Broadway theaters in New York City. It still stands next to the capitol building in central Havana, but much of the structure collapsed in the 1960s and has never been restored.

diva would soon step down from the Sonora Matancera, and she thought that Celia should take her place.

The mysterious messenger told Celia to go to Radio Progreso, ask for Rogelio Martínez—director of the Sonora Matancera—and inform him that Mr. Sotolongo had sent her to audition.

Celia might have been skeptical of that stranger who never used his first name, but she remembered her dream of the Campoamor stage and decided to play along. She met with Rogelio Martínez, who had joined the Sonora Matancera as a guitarist in 1926 and directed the group since 1932 (when Celia was seven). Now he offered her the chance to audition.

The dream was getting closer.

Celia woke up early on the morning of her first audition. She thought that she was the only one awake in her always-crowded family home, but Ollita got up earlier to brew Celia a cup of café con leche. (That's how Cuban kids usually learn how to drink coffee: a glass of warm milk, a splash of espresso, and a whole lot of sugar. It tastes like a comforting blend of coffee ice cream and delight. As kids get older the amount of warm milk gradually decreases, but the impressive helpings of sugar remain constant.)

Once caffeinated, Celia gathered up the sheet music for several different songs, put on a raincoat, and took an umbrella. It wasn't raining, but this was still the rainy season, so a sudden deluge could ambush her at any time. Celia wanted to be prepared for anything.

Luckily it didn't rain. She arrived at the studio bright and early, and the very first person she met there was a tall trumpet player named Pedro Knight.

Pedro had an easy smile and skin as dark as Celia's own. He had joined the Sonora Matancera in 1944—the year of the hurricane and the end of his stint playing music for a doomed circus. Now, six years later, he welcomed Celia Cruz to Radio Progreso.

Her audition didn't go very well, though.

The sheet music she brought with her had been arranged for an orchestra of fourteen musicians, and the Sonora Matancera only had nine. Celia joined their rehearsal anyway and sang along to a few of their regular numbers, but the combination didn't quite work.

Rogelio, the director, was still encouraging. He kept the sheet music that Celia had brought and promised to adapt those same songs to match the group's size and style. She could audition again when the new arrangements were ready for her.

Celia waited.

Weeks passed.

A newspaper article announced the departure of the great Myrta Silva and claimed that a singer named Celia Cruz had already been chosen to replace her. That would have been fantastic news if it was actually true, but Celia hadn't even had a proper audition yet. Meanwhile the premature announcement had the unintended consequence of making her abruptly unemployed; Celia's boss at Radio Cadena Suaritos fired her as soon as he read the paper.

Money was tight that summer. Celia needed work. She still hadn't heard back from the Sonora Matancera, and Rogelio Martínez wasn't returning her calls.

The days drained away. The dream seemed impossible.

Then, at the end of July, Celia finally got the phone call she had been waiting for. Rogelio told her that the musical arrangements were now properly arranged and that the band was ready to play for her second audition.

It went well this time.

Just a few days later, on the afternoon of August 3, 1950, Celia Cruz sang her debut performance as a member of the Sonora Matancera orchestra. Her whole family took up the front row of the studio audience, including her cousins: Nenita, who had insisted that Celia listen to the radio show, and Serafín, who had signed her up for her very first singing contest.

Serafín was especially thrilled and proud, but Celia's memory of his grin on that summer day would always be bittersweet. He died soon afterward, very suddenly. Serafín saw his young cousin become one of the most celebrated new singers in Havana, but he didn't live long enough to see her take on the rest of the Caribbean, the rest of Latin America, or the rest of the world.

Celia triumphed in part because her cousins looked out for her.

From a distance Celia's career might look like a straight shot skyward to inevitable stardom. Show business never ceases to be a struggle, however, and Celia's first year with the Sonora Matancera was anything but easy. Myrta Silva herself may have picked Celia as her successor, but Myrta's fans were still heartbroken. They missed her voice, which was higher than Celia's contralto. Some may have also been biased in favor of Myrta's appearance: Her skin was much lighter than Celia's. A campaign of phone calls and letters poured into Radio Progreso to demand the immediate cancellation of Celia Cruz.

Tía Ana remained a stalwart supporter, as always. She

told Celia to keep going, keep singing, and never bow her head to anyone.

Rogelio Martínez never regretted hiring Celia, and never wavered in his professional support of her voice. He wanted Celia to record new albums with the Sonora, so Rogelio went toe-to-toe with the recording executive Sydney Siegel, who would travel to Cuba for business. An American chauvinist with exclusive rights to record the Sonora Matancera orchestra with Seeco Records, Siegel insisted that female vocalists were only good for live performances and that a woman's place simply wasn't in the recording studio.

Rogelio couldn't change Siegel's mind until he finally offered to take on all the financial risk: If Celia's recordings didn't sell, then Siegel wouldn't have to pay the cost of making them. After the executive reluctantly agreed to this zero-risk investment, Celia made a short record with only two songs, one per side: "Cao, cao, maní picao" and "Mata siguaraya."

The record was a huge hit and sold all over the country.

The letter-writing campaign to cancel Celia fizzled away.

Sydney Siegel was suitably apologetic. For the next fifteen years, he would sign checks for more than seventy albums featuring Celia Cruz and the Sonora Matancera orchestra, and he never argued with Rogelio's creative decisions again

We all need our champions.

When Celia joined the Sonora, her sense of home and family expanded to include nine older brothers, every one of them supportive and fiercely protective. That band also knew more about Cuban musical history than practically anyone else on the island, and they gladly shared what they knew. Celia learned everything she could about the lighthearted joy of guarachas, the melancholy of boleros, the complex rhythms of rumbas, and the improvisational structure of sones. She learned dances born of carnaval and lyrics that mimicked the cries of street vendors in Havana. She mastered the music of home.

The Sonora Matancera had been touring all over Cuba for many years—usually by squeezing the entire band into a single Buick. Once, their car broke down on the way to the El Rincón sanctuary, a former leper colony in Santiago de Las Vegas where they had been hired to play for a festival on the eve of Saint Lazarus Day. Despite the occasion, they were unable to revive their Buick, so the band pushed that car for miles in their tuxedos. Luckily Santiago de Las Vegas isn't very far south of Havana.

After Celia's debut, the Sonora Matancera expanded their tours to include the whole Caribbean—and the whole Caribbean already knew who they were, thanks to the wide range and cultural reach of Havana's powerful radio stations. The Sonora played sold-out shows wherever they went.

Both at home and abroad, Celia's band of brothers were always quick to leap to her defense. Once while on tour, after the Sonora had performed for a particularly fancy and powerful crowd, an army general refused to leave Celia alone. The rest of the band noticed her frustration, stood by her side, and scared the general away. (Celia loved to tell that story later, but she refused to reveal the name of the humiliated general—or even the name of his country.)

Celia Cruz and the Sonora Matancera orchestra continued to flourish throughout the 1950s. They toured both together and apart. Celia also found sisterhood while singing accompaniment to the dance troupe Las Mulatas de Fuego. Whenever she toured solo, without the found family of her fellow performers, Celia relied on blood family and traveled with her cousin Nenita.

Back home in Havana she began to appear in films

and on television, performing everything from Coca-Cola jingles for TV commercials to nightclub music for movies set in Havana. Sometimes TV studio producers wanted another singer to lip-synch Celia's vocals, suggesting that someone with lighter skin should stand in front of the camera, but their whitewashing attempts never worked. No one ever believed that Celia's voice could possibly come from anyone else.

In 1957 Celia visited New York City for the first time. She was supposed to receive a gold record award from Sydney Siegel (the same guy who had tried to keep her out of recording just a few years earlier), but that show did not go according to plan.

The St. Nicholas Arena was absolutely packed—probably because they had oversold the tickets and squeezed too many people into too small a space—and then the police showed up.

Celia never knew exactly what happened, though she suspected that a rival club was jealous of the crowd at St. Nicholas and called in a noise complaint. The arrival of police officers sparked a small riot, and all plans for the evening collapsed in panicked screams. Celia herself was unsettled but unhurt. She vividly remembered seeing dozens of shoes left behind on the dance floor after her audience was forcibly escorted outside.

At the time, she felt understandably relieved to get out of New York and return to Havana, where they called her La Guarachera de Cuba. In 1957 the city and country of her birth still recognized Celia Cruz as a living symbol of Cuban musical identity.

All of that was about to change.

CHAPTER THREE

REVOLUTION AND EXILE

Celia's career ascended to undisputed stardom in the 1950s. Meanwhile, during that same decade, the country around her descended into chaos as two dictators wrestled for control of the island nation: "El General" Fulgencio Batista and "El Comandante" Fidel Castro.

BATISTA

CASTRO

Batista won the Cuban presidency twice. He was democratically elected the first time. The second time he led a military coup, seized presidential power, and canceled the elections of 1952. Corruption flourished under President Batista during that second term in office. Student riots and protest movements were brutally suppressed. His secret police murdered hundreds, possibly thousands, of people; the death toll varies wildly depending on who you ask.

In 1957, the same year that Celia survived a small riot in New York City, President Batista survived an assassination attempt. A student protest group stormed the presidential palace in Havana and took control of a station at the CMQ radio building where Celia had sung countless guarachas, boleros, and commercial jingles. The group planned to announce the death of President Batista over the airwaves, but neither the assassination nor the broadcast actually happened. Most of the would-be assassins and their co-conspirators were killed in the attempt.

Fidel Castro led a far more effective revolution. He also understood the power of radio, and he broadcast speeches on Radio Rebelde from dozens of secret stations. The conflict began in 1953 and ended on New Year's Eve in December 1958, when Batista fled the island and his government collapsed. Castro became prime minister, canceled the results of the 1958 elections, and brutally suppressed all political opposition. His firing squads murdered hundreds of people, and possibly thousands; the death toll varies wildly depending on who you ask.

Both of these men used brute force to seize and maintain power.

Both of them were fans of Celia Cruz.

Celia was not a fan of either.

In 1958, during the final year of Batista's rule, La Guarachera de Cuba focused her attention on the waning health of her mother rather than the waning health of her country.

Ollita's doctor diagnosed her worsening illness as cancer, which shook the foundations of Celia's world. She needed to make sure that her mother got the best medical care possible, which meant that she needed to make more money, which paradoxically meant that Celia needed to leave her mother's side. Performing in Mexico City paid better than shows in Havana.

Celia was touring in Mexico when President Batista fled Cuba. Revolutionaries led by Castro came down from the mountains to assume control. She rushed back home to Havana and found the city in turmoil. Men with guns were strutting everywhere. Most of her hometown had shut down completely. No one had the slightest idea what was going to happen next.

The new government immediately seized every radio and television station. Airwaves filled with propaganda rather than dance music. It became increasingly difficult for Celia, the Sonora, and every other musician in Havana to find work—and Celia needed to work. She accepted a rare invitation to perform at a private party hosted by Miguel Ángel Quevedo—the wealthy publisher of *Bohemia* magazine.

El Comandante himself arrived at the party while she was in mid-song.

The host offered to make introductions: "Celia, Fidel wants to meet you. He says that he used to clean his gun to your song 'Burundanga' while he was in the mountains."

Celia politely refused. "If that man wants to meet me, let him come to me."

Fidel took the hint and kept his distance.

Soon after the party, however, Celia was informed that she would be *required* to sing at the Blanquita Theater. After the first rehearsal for this mandatory show, the director told the gathered musicians that Cuba's new leader would be in attendance and that all of them were expected to show him the utmost respect.

During the show, right before Celia stepped onstage, she was further informed that she would have to sing "Burundanga," Fidel Castro's favorite gun-cleaning song.

Celia refused. She switched up the program. The back-up musicians all supported her, showing more loyalty to La Guarachera than to El Comandante.

After that performance Celia hurried backstage, where the director told her that she wouldn't be getting a paycheck. She had failed to show proper respect for the new regime.

Celia politely informed him that she preferred her own self-respect to his money.

She still needed to pay for Ollita's cancer treatments, though.

She needed to find work.

She needed to sing.

Sanctuary in Mexico City looked more and more appealing.

The power struggle between Celia Cruz and Fidel Castro continued to escalate.

Celia had already become far more than a singer; she was a living symbol of Cuban culture as a whole. Cuba's new leader wanted to prove the legitimacy of his rule by publicly demonstrating control over Celia herself. Fidel needed her to sing for him. He refused to take no for an answer.

El Comandante sent a steady stream of agents to Celia's house, each with an official summons to a state event where she would be expected to perform. Celia sent her brother, Bárbaro, to answer each knock at the door while she hid in a closet. Bárbaro smoothly lied to every heavily armed agent of the regime and said that his sister was not at home.

That lie needed to be true.

Celia needed to get out of town.

As the decade ended it became increasingly clear that freedom of artistic expression would not be valued highly by the Castro regime. Musicians played for Fidel, or they did not play at all.

Mexican theaters and nightclubs reached out to both Celia and the Sonora Matancera, offering steady work to all of them, but the orchestra needed official permission to leave the country—and that permission was becoming increasingly difficult to find.

Rogelio Martínez began the bureaucratically hostile process of getting exit visas for everyone in the Sonora.

Celia began the emotionally wrenching process of leaving her mother—again—this time surrounded by even more medical uncertainty and political turmoil.

Ollita freely offered her blessing. "Go," she said. "Don't worry about me. Your future is calling you."

Celia packed her bags. She waited for Rogelio to call, just as she had waited exactly ten years earlier, in July 1950, when he finally phoned to say that the musical arrangements were ready for her audition.

Another family crisis struck while Celia waited: her *father's* health suddenly and dramatically worsened. Ollita still hoped to recover from her illness, but doctors told Simón Cruz that he would not live for very much longer.

This proud and stoic man had never been close to his joyful daughter. In fact, as far as Celia could tell, the man had never been close to anyone. Even after they made their peace, her father still maintained his distance. Now the two of them said goodbye, both knowing that they would probably never meet again if Celia boarded a plane for Mexico City.

He kept his promise not to hold her back.

She offered support by making all the arrangements for his looming funeral and paying every expense in advance.

The waiting continued.

Ollita waited to get better.

Simón waited to get worse.

Celia waited for a phone call.

She finally got it on July 14, 1960, when Rogelio called to say that he had visas and plane tickets ready for the very next day. The Castro regime had granted permission for the Sonora Matancera orchestra to go on tour—as long as they promised to come right back.

Fidel Castro hated to lose. As a boy he threw tantrums and beat his forehead against the nearest wall every time he lost a ball game. The grown man with the same temperament would never graciously accept defeat in his battle of wills against Celia Cruz. El Comandante still needed to demonstrate his dominance over all things Cuban: the government, the people, the culture, and the living embodiment of musical Cubanity, Celia Cruz.

Why, then, did he let her leave the country?

Did the dictator have a sudden change of heart?

Did he believe that she would owe him a debt of gratitude after he granted this apparently gracious favor?

Regardless of his reasons, Fidel Castro would soon be able to exploit new kinds of leverage against Celia. She could tour with the Sonora, but the rest of her family would remain in Havana. The Castro regime controlled the national border that would soon separate Celia Cruz from everyone she loved most.

Celia stayed up late joking with her siblings the night before the Sonora went back on tour. She woke up early on July 15, 1960, and shared strong, sweet coffee with her beloved Ollita. Celia promised to be back in Havana by Nochebuena dinner on Christmas Eve, and at the time both of them believed it.

Most of the family joined Celia at the airport to see her

off—everyone except for her father. Either Simón felt too sick to leave the house or else he simply preferred to say his goodbyes quietly and in private. The rest of the family was loud. They laughed, cried, hugged, and waved their arms around, taking up the whole airline terminal with boisterous affection; in other words, they acted like many Cuban families saying farewell to one of their own. Tía Ana

solemnly swore that she would take good care of Ollita and keep her company at every medical appointment.

Rogelio finally interrupted all that family noise to gather the Sonora together. He explained the many ways that the customs process had recently changed, making absolutely sure that no one in the orchestra got detained on a technicality.

All of them made it through customs. The band left the terminal and crossed the runway on foot. Caribbean sunlight filled the whole sky. Celia turned back to see her mamá and tía watching her from the observation deck, blew a kiss for both of them, then boarded the plane.

She would never see her mother again.

First the sight of Havana vanished behind them, and then the whole island disappeared. Only sea and sky were visible outside. The Sonora Matancera orchestra had officially left Cuban airspace to fly over international waters, so now it was safe to freely discuss the brutal truth that this would be a one-way trip.

Rogelio confessed that he intended to stay in Mexico and asked the others to stay with him.

Celia sat next to Pedro Knight, the tall trumpet player who had gradually become her dearest friend in the close-knit

Sonora. She squeezed his hand hard. If her long nails left any marks on his skin when the two of them shared the wrenching first instant of exile, then he bore it without complaint.

On that day, and in the days that followed, Celia's

awareness of exile settled into her stomach like a swallowed knife and stayed there. Only singing eased the constant pain. She found solace and belonging onstage, right where she had left them.

Celia poured everything she was and everything she knew into her voice—and her voice was in high demand. Both Celia and the Sonora Matancera may have stalled in their careers back home, unable to find steady work without the official approval of the regime, but now they found themselves booked to perform every night of the week.

Only a few of those busy weeks passed before Celia learned that her father was dead.

She had known it would happen soon, but she still wasn't prepared.

Celia grieved for her papi. She grieved for the emotional distance and misunderstandings that had long kept them apart. She grieved for the physical distance between herself and the funeral that she had carefully planned but could not attend. Her father's death took the knife of exile and twisted it hard.

Celia sang harder. That was her sanctuary. As a musical superhero she needed the exact opposite of a Fortress of Solitude, and she found it in the crowded, sold-out nightclubs and theaters of Mexico City, where her voice gave shape to songs of home.

Back home, Fidel Castro grew impatient. He declared that every Cuban citizen abroad would have their citizenship revoked permanently if they did not return to the island by October.

Come back.

Come home.

Beg me to let you back in before I change the locks.

Celia never bowed her head to anyone.

She refused to go back and remained in exile with the Sonora Matancera.

The whole Sonora Matancera ended up renting apartments in the same building in Mexico City. They began to rebuild a sense of community together.

Celia had already thought of her Sonora bandmates as brothers. Now exile strengthened those familial bonds *and* added a whole bunch of new cousins as their apartment building filled with more and more exiled musicians. She was grateful, though she also understood in practical terms that this precarious sense of home and fellowship would be temporary—especially as far as the building itself was concerned. Noncitizens of Mexico could not legally own Mexican property of any kind in 1960, and Celia was not a Mexican citizen. Displaced and stateless by Fidel's decree, she no longer held any kind of citizenship.

The bureaucratic process of becoming a naturalized citizen of Mexico was notoriously difficult. Celia tried, and made very little progress. She started to think about making a new home somewhere farther north. Then things got complicated with another member of the Sonora Matancera.

Pedro Knight was one of Celia's closest friends, and he had been ever since the day she first tried to audition for the orchestra, but Celia had long ago promised herself that she would never fall in love with a fellow musician. Pedro's conduct back in Havana had seemed like a pretty good argument in favor of keeping that promise. The man had been married and divorced twice already, and during the decade of their friendship Celia counted no fewer than eleven girlfriends. She had zero interest in becoming the twelfth—at least until exile changed everything for both of them.

It started on the plane, when Celia and Pedro each instinctively reached for the other's hand when Rogelio confessed that there would be no turning back.

It continued in Mexico City, where Pedro was the only one who could still make Celia laugh.

The two of them told each other pretty much everything, so it made perfect sense for Pedro to ask Celia's advice when he realized that he was falling in love with his closest friend.

Celia said that he should tell her.

Pedro confessed that he was scared.

Celia insisted that if this girl really was his closest friend, then she probably already knew. Pedro should trust her.

That was the moment when the two friends became something more.

The two somehow kept their new relationship an absolute secret, despite living in an apartment complex stuffed full of homesick Cuban musicians starved for any kind of gossip whatsoever.

Celia and Pedro continued to keep their secret while the Sonora toured throughout Mexico as part of a whole caravan of acts and entertainers, barely finding the time to eat between sets. It was exhausting, but the whirlwind of constant performance also sustained Celia. Nothing else could stitch the open wound of exile—not stolen moments with Pedro, or weekly phone calls home to Ollita. Mother and daughter cautiously shared their news, aware that the telephone lines were almost certainly bugged.

Ollita's voice sounded noticeably weaker.

Celia poured more strength into her own.

She sang for film stars and politicians at a private party,

where she met the Mexican president Gustavo Díaz Ordaz. President Ordaz was delighted by her performance. He refrained from demanding that Celia sing any song in particular and later sent her the gift of a fancy watch engraved with the words "Para la voz de Cuba."

For Cuba's voice.

Mexico showed hospitality to the Sonora Matancera, but Celia still felt unsettled and adrift. She loved Mexico City. She loved the community of exiles she had helped to build there. She was also making decent money, performing constantly and recording new albums, but Celia remained unable to use any of her earnings to make a down payment on a place of her own.

She kept thinking about cities farther north.

In July 1961, a full year after leaving Havana behind, Celia accepted a short-term solo contract from the Palladium theater in Los Angeles. She traveled alone, without any distractions from her tall trumpet player, and found clarity in that solitude.

Her Mexican travel documents expired. That made it temporarily impossible for her to return, but Celia didn't really mind. She understood what she wanted, and where she needed to go next.

Celia accepted another contract from another Palladium theater—this time in New York City.

CHAPTER FOUR

KNIGHTHOOD IN NEW YORK

Cuba and the United States did not get along very well in the year 1961.

First the United States supported a counterrevolution against Castro's new regime. The CIA aided more than a thousand Cuban exiles who tried to fight their way home by invading Girón Beach, close to the Bay of Pigs. American support was not much help, however, and the invasion failed.

Fidel Castro responded by declaring Cuba a socialist republic allied to the Soviet Union. He asked for Russian military protection to prevent any more invasion attempts fostered by the United States. Russia agreed. The resulting standoff between superpowers in the Caribbean nearly started a global nuclear war.

The United States also blockaded Cuba with a trade embargo, forbidding business of any kind between the neighboring nations. That sounds a lot less terrifying than a nuclear apocalypse, but the embargo still had devastating effects; this unsuccessful attempt to hurt the Cuban government succeeded in hurting the Cuban people. Goods no longer traveled freely between the island and the mainland, and neither did music. Centuries-old conversations and collaborations between the musicians of Havana, New Orleans, and New York City suddenly fell silent.

Havana also suffered from another kind of silence. Exiled musicians had more than their bodies banished from Cuba. They were also erased from the island's musical history, their sheet music shredded and recordings destroyed—which included every album featuring Celia Cruz.

The voice of Cuba had been banned from Cuba.

Castro's voice resounded. *If you will not sing for me, then you will not sing at all.*

New York was still listening to Celia, though the city also felt like an alien planet to the girl from Santos Suárez. Skyscrapers loomed above her like the fingers of a massive hand, and she couldn't tell if that hand intended to hold her up or close in a fist all around her.

Celia cautiously settled into a tiny apartment and started to learn English, the better to communicate with local hairdressers. They were experts at styling Black hair, which was nice, but Celia did not enjoy the helpless, voiceless feeling of being unable to speak to someone who held the fate of her hair in their hands.

That first winter in New York came as a shock. The sight of falling snow was magical, but the cold made her ears feel like they were going to break off and shatter when they hit the sidewalk.

Celia kept warm as best she could and poured the warmth of her voice into the ears of New York City. She started to feel cautiously welcome in that chilly world of endless concrete, helped in no small part by a seismic shift in US immigration law: Cuban refugees were now permitted to apply for permanent residence in the United States.

Always a magnetic force of community and fellowship, Celia gathered more of the Cuban diaspora around her—including the Sonora Matancera, which left Mexico behind and followed Celia to New York City. Once they got the band back together, Celia immediately moved in with Pedro, the tall trumpet player. Rogelio Martínez was a bit shocked—not by their relationship, but by the fact that the two of them had managed to keep it a secret for so long.

The Sonora was soon hired by the Puerto Rico Theater in the Bronx, so the band settled in to do what they did best. Rogelio, disciplined taskmaster of musical excellence that he was, made all of them rehearse daily until they found their shared flow again. Celia and Pedro escaped when they could and took road trips outside the city, which felt more and more like home every time they turned the car around to come back. They managed to make it work as professional musicians in New York City, which is no small accomplishment in any decade. Celia earned enough to keep sending money home for Ollita's medical care.

In April 1962, the night before the Sonora's debut performance at the Puerto Rico Theater, Celia had a dream about her mother.

"Don't forget that I'll always be with you," Ollita told her in the dream.

Celia woke smiling, thrilled to have dreamed a glimpse of her mom and full of the simmering excitement that she always felt right before opening night. She went to get her nails done, savored their expressive elegance on the tips of her fingertips, and hummed a tune on her way back to the apartment.

Pedro was on the phone when she got there. His back was turned. His tone of voice was grave. He didn't notice Celia when she opened the door. She was just about to call out to him when she heard Pedro say that Ollita had died in the night, and that he didn't know how to tell Celia the news.

Before we learn about Celia's shock and grief in that moment, we should talk about something.

Celia Cruz always believed in the cathartic honesty of feeling and sharing the way that she actually felt. This does not mean she lacked control. Note how well she kept her romance with Pedro a secret in Mexico City, despite living in a crowded apartment building full of gossip-starved and homesick musicians. Note the poise and diplomacy of her disgusted refusal to sing Fidel Castro's favorite song. Celia had discipline, discretion, and a keen sense of privacy—none of which contradicts the power of emotional authenticity that burned like the light of ten thousand suns every time she stepped onstage.

Celia Cruz believed in feeling the way she actually felt.

When she heard that her beloved Ollita had died, Celia screamed.

Pedro could not console her. Friends and neighbors could not console her. The rest of the Sonora Matancera rushed over and did their best to console her. Celia was having none of it. She cried out Ollita's name, over and over again, unable to say any other word—at least until Pedro suggested that they cancel the show that night. How could anyone expect Celia to perform when the foundations of her world had just shattered?

She was having none of that, either. Celia silenced any and all discussion of canceling the Sonora's opening night in New York City. She needed to sing. She needed the sanctuary that she only ever found onstage, and she found it at the Puerto Rico Theater in the Bronx.

The Sonora Matancera knew the history of Cuban music better than anyone. That history was still happening, despite the brutal silences of embargo and state censorship enforced by both governments. That history would continue to unfold in both nations as ancestral riffs and rhythms haunted new instruments. One powerful moment in musical history happened on April 7, 1962, when Celia shared her fierce joy with the gathered crowd and hid backstage to sob between songs.

The following day, on April 8, La Guarachera de Cuba resumed her battle of wills with El Comandante. Celia Cruz formally asked for the regime's permission to attend her mother's funeral in Havana.

Fidel Castro never forgave Celia for her refusal to sing, or for her refusal to return to Cuba at his command. Now he took his revenge and refused her request.

Dictators are nothing if not petty.

Celia believed in feeling the way that she actually felt. She was not allowed to attend Ollita's distant funeral, and on that day she felt rage and despair to a degree that she had never known before.

Celia Cruz vowed to never set foot on Cuban soil for as long as Fidel Castro lived.

New York became home. Celia and Pedro were both determined to make it their home, and the city itself seemed determined to welcome them. Soon after Ollita's death her daughter became the first Latina to ever perform at Carnegie Hall.

Celia and Pedro got married that same summer. The two of them wed in a simple civil ceremony on July 14, almost exactly two years after they went into exile together.

Celia was Catholic, but marrying in the church required baptismal certificates that remained lost in Cuba, so instead of an ornate ceremony, her marriage to Pedro began with the quiet intimacy of vows spoken in a judge's chambers. It was all they wanted or needed in that moment. Afterward they ate at a local diner.

Celia continued to find and build community with her fellow refugees. The Castro regime referred to the whole diaspora of Cuban exiles as gusanos, which means "worms." Celia called them family.

Concerned about her sister Gladys, who had always been determined to speak her mind—a dangerous trait in Castro's Havana—Celia successfully arranged for her younger sister to travel from Cuba to Mexico, and from there helped Gladys find asylum in New York.

Ollita was gone. Family remained, fragmentary but thriving.

Celia's career also continued to thrive. She took more risks onstage, improvising new lyrics whenever moved by the music and the moment. She took stock of where she had been, where she had landed, and what she wanted to do next.

Celia's contract with Seeco Records was exclusive. It specified that Celia Cruz could only record with the Sonora Matancera. She still adored her orchestral family, but she felt creatively stifled by filling their albums with the same classic songs, over and over again. Celia wanted to also work with other musicians and create new collaborations.

Sydney Siegel—the same man who had refused to let Celia record *any* albums until Rogelio finally wore him down—now begged her to stay with Seeco Records. She gently declined. Mr. Siegel wept when he signed her contract release.

Celia and the Sonora continued to tour throughout the country and the world—sometimes together, but increasingly apart. Pedro Knight still played trumpet for the Sonora Matancera, and their touring schedule took him farther and farther away from Celia. The newlyweds did their best to meet in distant cities whenever possible, but it wasn't enough. This was not the life they had chosen when they shared quiet vows in the judge's chambers.

Pedro had been married twice before. Both times he chose music over marriage. This time he set the trumpet aside, left the Sonora Matancera orchestra with Rogelio's sad blessing, and vowed to support Celia's career over his own. Pedro finally earned the knighthood of his name.

Celia Cruz swore the oath of American citizenship in a Brooklyn courthouse in 1961, ending her long years as a stateless citizen of nowhere at all. She used her voice to remake her community, her family, and her home more than a thousand miles north of the old neighborhood in the south of Havana. She rebuilt a sense of belonging that her most dangerous fan had tried to confiscate.

"In exile," she said, "I have learned to be Cuban in a way that might not have been possible if I had stayed in Cuba."

When Celia left that Brooklyn courthouse with natural-ization papers in hand, she screamed for joy.

CHAPTER FIVE

AZÚCAR AND SALSA

Released in 1974, the album *Celia & Johnny* lives in many different places on the internet, easily available on different streaming sites.

The album also lives in record stores, still circulating in CD and vinyl.

The album lives.

Celia & Johnny is the first recorded collaboration between Celia Cruz and Johnny Pacheco, the Dominican-born musician, composer, producer, and cofounder of Fania Records.

On the front cover Johnny holds one of Celia's hands in both of his, deferential and delighted to be working with the Voice of Cuba. Celia smiles beside him like a proudly indulgent tía. On the flip side of the original album cover, they sit back to back. The picture on the back of the reissued CD case shows the two of them onstage instead, much older and both laughing.

"Química" is the first track on the album, and Celia had to argue with the record producers to keep it there. She insisted that the lyrics by young songwriter Junior Cepeda beautifully dramatized a conversation held between different sets of drums.

No one knows exactly what the word *química* means. Most agree that it came from one of the many African languages forced to join the chorus of the Caribbean as a result of the slave trade. Best guesses insist that the word describes a life well lived, a way of walking that becomes a dance, and a way of dancing that combines abandon with precision.

Find the song and listen. Pay close attention to how Celia illustrates and embodies that half-glimpsed definition of *química* as she repeats the word over and over again. Try to keep up with her flawless enunciation. All three syllables are as bright and precise as hummingbirds zooming between flowers to drink nectar, every repetition of the full word as playful as a wave at the beach that knocks you over.

Johnny's voice offers support. Celia doesn't need it. His vocals drop out. Trumpets kick in, fanfare and heraldry for what comes next. Celia sings about the song itself for a bit. Then, one minute and twenty-two seconds into the track, she suddenly says, "¡Azúcar!"

That word arrives with a growl and a grin, like Celia means to take a bite out of the microphone right there in the recording studio. She says it as though summoning the taste of victory cake, her winning prize from that first singing contest in Havana. She says it like the word belongs to her. She also says it like a gift and a secret that now belongs to you.

Azúcar is Spanish for "sugar."

In Celia's voice it means much more than that.

This is how she told the story:

Celia was in Miami, eating with friends at one of her favorite Cuban restaurants. (She was *always* surrounded by close friends. Celia made friends everywhere, and she held those friendships dearly.) After an excellent meal that still wasn't nearly as good as Ollita's ropa vieja, Celia ordered coffee.

The young waiter asked if she wanted sugar.

Celia was stunned by the question. How could anyone ask a Cuban lady speaking Cuban-accented Spanish in a Cuban restaurant if she wanted sugar in her coffee?

She smiled and leaned forward. Years of training as a teacher kicked in, because this was a teachable moment.

"Look, chico," she said to the young waiter. "You know Cuban coffee is really strong and bitter. So give it to me with azúúúcar!" Everyone at the table laughed at the extra vowels that Celia poured into that word.

CAFÉ CUBANO

CUBAN COFFEE usually refers to milk-free shots of stovetop espresso mixed with thick sugar syrup. You make the syrup by stirring the first scalding-hot drops of espresso into a sizable spoonful of cane sugar. This kind of cafecito is the drink that Celia ordered in her favorite Miami restaurant. This is also the drink that she sipped every morning when Pedro brought a fresh cup of café cubano to her bedside.

CAFÉ CON LECHE is a big glass of warm milk sweetened by an entire milkshake's worth of sugar and mixed with a modest amount of espresso. This is the drink that Ollita made for Celia when she was a kid.

The CORTADO is the odd cousin in the Cuban coffee family, sweetened with a dollop of milk rather than a spoonful of sugar; lactose in the milk caramelizes slightly when it hits the hot espresso, so technically sugar is still involved. This is often the preferred form of coffee for Cubans with diabetes.

The PECADO is the most powerfully indulgent cousin in the café cubano family. The word means both "sin" and "espresso mixed with sweet condensed milk." Cuban character Abuela Claudia invokes this sweetest sin in both the stage and the screen versions of *In the Heights* by Lin-Manuel Miranda and Quiara Alegría Hudes.

> For recipes of all four, read *The Cuban Table: A Celebra-*
> *tion of Food, Flavors, and History* by Ana Sofía Peláez
> and Ellen Silverman.

Celia told the restaurant story during her performance that same night, in between sets, because it continued to be a teachable moment. The whole audience laughed hard at the way she poured her whole voice into that one-word punch line.

Her audience demanded to hear the restaurant story again on the following night. The same thing happened on the night after that. They couldn't get enough of the story, and Celia got tired of repeating it, so eventually she condensed the whole anecdote down to a single word and just shouted, "¡AZÚCAR!"

Her audience immediately leaped to their feet and roared applause.

Celia threw sugar into pretty much every show and album after that.

Imagine that first moment, on that Miami stage, when Celia provoked an instantaneous standing ovation with a single word. *Azúcar* meant so much more to that crowd than mere coffee sweetener. It means so much more than *sugar* when Celia invokes it in "Químbara," where *azúcar* joins the title to describe a life well lived, a way of walking that becomes a dance, and a way of dancing that combines abandon with precision.

Azúcar insists that life is a carnival, even in exile.

Azúcar performs on opening night despite overwhelming waves of grief that come crashing backstage in between every song.

Azúcar finds joy in sorrow, and it makes the sorrows sing.

Azúcar means savoring the bitter with the sweet.

Celia was always a teacher. She understood the full weight of sugar in her own life and family, in the lifeblood of her island home, and in the blood shed throughout centuries of colonial domination. That bitter history is why Celia's audience jumped to their feet in Miami. Because the story of sugar in the Caribbean is also the story of slavery.

Christopher Columbus brought sugarcane on his second voyage across the Atlantic. To harvest the cane he enslaved the Carib and Taíno people of the islands, slandering them as cannibals to make their enslavement more palatable to Queen Isabella in Spain. Sugar production devoured the lives of Native Nation citizens in the Caribbean just as hungrily as Europe devoured the sugar that they harvested. That same hunger fueled the transatlantic slave trade. Cane sugar became the white gold of Havana's wealth, coveted by Spain, by England, and (eventually) by the young United States.

As a child, Celia heard war stories told by her grandfather, a mambí veteran of the fight for Cuban independence against Spanish colonial rule. As a young radio star, she toured throughout Cuba with the Sonora Matancera and played for private parties at former plantations. As a lifelong student—and teacher—of Cuban musical history and culture, she knew that the Afro-Caribbean traditions she mastered were born of diaspora.

Celia also had more personal and immediate reasons to be wary of sugar, because her husband was diabetic. She paid close attention to Pedro's blood sugar and insisted on cooking for him in order to keep him safe. Pedro used plenty of the sweet stuff to prepare Celia's cup of café cubano every morning, but for medical reasons he couldn't stir sugar into his own coffee. Celia joked that her azúcar was the only kind that he was allowed to have.

She knew that sugar was dangerous. She knew that the

history of sugar was murderous. She was an authority on the music that had grown out of that same history, and she sprinkled azúcar in songs of loss and heartbreak as well as songs of joy and celebration. To invoke Caribbean sugar is to savor and acknowledge both the bitter and the sweet.

Celia worked hard to ensure that the past, present, and future kept talking to one another, and she did so throughout her entire career. Singing classics from the island was not just an expression of nostalgia for her lost home; as a Black Cuban woman in exile, she understood herself to be a member of more than one diaspora. From the moment when young Celia sat and listened to her neighbors sing in Lucumi to the moment when she recorded "Yo viviré," the very last track on her very last album, Celia knew that the music of ancestry was an act of survival.

As a radio star she studied son, rumba, cha-cha, bolero, mambo, danzón—any and every form of Afro-Cuban music she could find. She studied Lucumi music and language with Obdulio Morales, the santero bandleader at the Tropicana nightclub, and she recorded songs of praise to the Lucumi pantheon of orishas with the Sonora Matancera.

In the early 1950s Celia headlined the Sun Sun Ba Baé,

a celebration of Afro-Cuban culture that included Lucumí lyrics. She learned that the title song probably meant "beautiful bird of the dawn," though some insisted that *sun sun* meant "owl" instead. When Celia performed "Sun sun ba baé," she either honored a bird that sings at day-break or a bird that hunts at night—a beginning, an ending, or both at once.

She also wondered if "sun sun" referred to "zun zun," the Cuban name for the smallest bird on earth. Decades later and more than a thousand miles north of the zun zun's native habitat, Celia would teach Big Bird about the tiny hummingbird while guest-starring on *Sesame Street*. She was always a teacher, and she was always mindful of the past while speaking to the future.

In Spanish the word *salsa* means "sauce." In supermarkets throughout the United States, salsa refers to mild, medium, or hot sauce for dipping chips or mixing with bean dishes and stews. As a genre of music, the meaning of salsa is hotly contested.

When Johnny Pacheco first launched Fania Records in 1964, he started to call all kinds of Cuban dance music by the same saucy name.

Tito Puente, Puerto Rican monarch of mambo and expert on all kinds of traditional Cuban music, absolutely hated that name. "What salsa?" Tito would complain to Celia. "You eat salsa, you don't dance to it."

Celia laughed and sympathized with Tito. She didn't even like the taste of spicy food, despite all the times her Mexican friends had tried to share their magnificent cooking. "I don't like to suffer while I'm eating!" she told them. Notwithstanding that aversion to edible salsa, Celia still appreciated what Johnny Pacheco was up to. The albums she had recorded with the great Tito Puente were not selling well. Music she loved, lived, and breathed was becoming endangered in the United States.

Rock and roll filled concert halls in the 1970s. Disco

took over the dance floor. Immigrant kids coming of age in the United States were trying to fit in, caught between worlds, and the new world was much louder. Young Cuban Americans drifted away from the musical nostalgia of their exiled parents and grandparents.

It's not exactly surprising that different generations would have different tastes in dance music. Styles change. Every new generation invents new steps and new ways to move through the world. To exiled Cubanity, however, this felt more like amnesia than innovation. The almost-forgotten boleros, guarachas, and pregoneros were more than dance tunes from days gone by. That music captured the voices of home—sometimes literally.

Los pregoneros were Cuban street vendors who sang about their wares; the word sometimes translates as "town crier." A pregón is a cry, a sales pitch put to music.

Margarita Engle's memoir-in-verse, *Enchanted Air*, describes childhood visits to Cuba and the sight of an older cousin dancing to the song of an ice cream seller. Her picture book *A Song of Frutas* also dramatizes the singing of a Cuban street vendor.

Beny Moré, another renowned Cuban singer, worked as a pregonero when he first arrived in Havana at the age of seventeen. His day job as an aspiring musician was to sing the praises of bruised fruit that he peddled from a street cart.

After the revolution Beny stayed in Havana, but he didn't live for very much longer. His liver gave out on him in 1963, when Beny was just forty-three years old. Meanwhile the Castro regime outlawed pregoneros, abruptly ending an old tradition and silencing the choral voices of Cuban cities. This new restriction may or may not have happened because pregoneros reminded Fidel of Celia Cruz. In the early days of her radio career, she was best known for singing pregónes like "El yerbero moderno" (based on the sales pitches of grocers peddling fresh basil) and "El pregón del pescador" (which means "The Fishmonger's Cry").

In 1973, ten years after the death of Beny Moré, Celia performed alongside several other exiled musicians in a tribute concert dedicated to the late, great singer. Celia couldn't help but notice that the crowd who gathered for

that concert was composed entirely of elders. No one had been able to coax their kids into showing up.

The voices of home were fading away.

Celia first recorded "El yerbero moderno" with the Sonora Matancera in the early 1950s. She rerecorded the exact same song with Johnny Pacheco in 1974, only now it was salsa instead of a pregón, and suddenly everyone wanted to hear it. Multigenerational audiences flocked to salsa concerts. Elders joined their grandkids on the dance floor.

The voices of the past still had a future.

Other Latin American genres of music got chopped up and added to the sauce, which made purists like Tito Puente increasingly grumpy. Tito mourned the disappearance of something he considered essential: the names and identities of individual traditions, lost when Johnny's record label turned all of them into salsa.

Celia still refused to eat spicy food, but she also insisted that salsa helped to save those distinct traditions from extinction. Immigrants are often pressured to change their names into something that new neighbors find easier to pronounce; now the music that Celia loved, lived, and breathed was surviving and thriving in the United States under a new name.

Fidel didn't like that new name, either, which Celia very much enjoyed. The official line of the Castro regime was that salsa music did not exist: The word was nothing more than a cheap marketing ploy. Cuban musicians officially sanctioned by the regime did not play salsa. One such band, the Orquesta Aragón, toured "real Cuban music" throughout Latin America—including Venezuela, where Celia and Johnny happened to be putting on a salsa performance at the same hotel. After midnight the Aragón gave up on their empty room, packed up their instruments, and joined Celia's crowded ballroom audience instead.

The word *salsa*, to be clear, *was* a marketing ploy. Fania rebranded Cuban dance music in order to sell more records and concert tickets, and it worked. Celia's use of this new musical genre was more community-minded than mercenary, however. In every album she made sure to include bombas for Puerto Ricans and merengues for Dominicans alongside the guarachas that she recorded for her fellow Cubans. She collaborated with mariachis while singing local favorites in Mexico. Celia made sure that salsa did not simply consume each formerly distinct flavor of Latin music. Instead she celebrated a broader, more expansive sense of shared Latinidad.

"The music gave us mutual cause," said the legendary

Willie Colón about salsa's expansive reach. "It made us visible to each other."

Celia Cruz was crowned La Reina de Salsa by legions of devoted fans, and as the Queen of Salsa, she ruled wisely and well.

This chapter of Celia's story celebrates messy translations. She spoke English, but she also felt very self-conscious about her strong accent and joked that her "English isn't very good-looking." She almost never sang in that language. Celia stuck to Spanish lyrics, occasional Lucumi, and her own improvised, scat-like lyrics—a gift that she accepted from jazz and translated into salsa. One of the very few exceptions to her musical avoidance of English happened on *Sesame Street* in 1994, when Celia performed an English adaptation of Fidel Castro's favorite song accompanied by a chorus of muppets. That may or may not have been a playful jab at her dangerous fan.

The word *salsa* makes a mess in translation. It meant "money" to Fania Records and "sauce" to the mambo king Tito Puente. Celia took that disputed word and made it mean "survival" for the displaced and stateless music of her heart and home.

She translated the Spanish word for "sugar" into something as public as an anthem and as private as a whispered promise.

The definition of *química* may remain a mystery, but when Celia sings it, her meaning is clear.

Find the song, and listen again.

Let her voice teach you the many meanings of *química* and *azúcar*.

CHAPTER SIX

HER ROYAL MAJESTY

Queen Celia Cruz reigned over the final third of the twentieth century, and her stage presence was everything that anyone could ever want from royalty. Her performances offered loving kindness mixed with incandescent radiance, as though your favorite tía had somehow become the sun and the moon and the stars.

Every aspect of her style grew brighter and more flamboyant as the years passed. Celia wore larger wigs and higher heels with pride, continued to delight in the elegant

nails that had gotten in the way of her early piano lessons, and shimmered onstage in gowns covered with whole galaxies of sequins. The sight of her was a celebration.

Celia's warmth never faded behind all that glamour. She continued to be the loving, genuine, authentically open-hearted singer who poured fierce joy into every song, and audiences adored her for it.

Weather could not slow her down. Celia performed outdoors in thunderstorms, rolls of thunder adding to the wild applause from rain-drenched crowds. She hated to disappoint anyone by canceling a show.

Once she broke an ankle while descending from a concert stage. She had no time to see a doctor before the next performance. Celia sang right through that excruciating pain and translated it into music, just like she always did.

Immediately after X-rays confirmed the broken bone and doctors wrapped her ankle in a cast, Celia put on another show. The plaster cast finished drying under stage lights. After that, Enrique Arteaga, Celia's clothing designer, made special boots out of shining gold lamé that could fit over the cast. She flew to the Dominican Republic for her next show and proudly wore those golden boots onstage.

When Celia performed for carnaval in Tenerife, the largest of the Canary Islands, she was amazed to see an ocean-size crowd in attendance. Hundreds of thousands of people had gathered together, breaking world records for the largest concert audience in history. Celia offered "Bemba colorá" to that vast ocean of people, and the sound of the crowd singing right along with her seemed to hold up the whole sky.

Celia took her responsibility on the stage very seriously," said Marc Anthony, her esteemed colleague in salsa. "It was amazing to see her sitting backstage quietly and serenely before it was her time to go on. From the instant that orchestra played the first chord, she became this gigantic presence. She never, ever disappointed her audience."

Cuban superstar Gloria Estefan agreed: "Celia stepped onstage, and it's like the world stood still."

Celia balanced the extravagant spectacle of her performances with private rituals and familiar routines that helped her transform every new hotel room into a temporary home. Like many live performers she was very superstitious, avoiding hotel rooms marked with the number thirteen and forbidding anyone from ever whistling in her dressing room.

The first thing Celia always did whenever she arrived at a new hotel was to pick up extra stationery from the front desk so she could write letters to friends and family. She never forgot a birthday or an anniversary, always remembered to send Christmas cards, and wrote constant letters to all the nieces and nephews she had accumulated—some related by blood, others born to dear friends, and all of them semi-adopted by Celia Cruz.

Whenever she settled into a new room, Celia first called her sister Gladys in New York to let her know that she had safely arrived. Next Celia would set up a small altar with a rosary, images of the saints—especially Saint Christopher, the patron of safe travels—and framed pictures of Gladys's kids. Later, when Celia returned to her hotel room after the show, she wanted those family pictures to be the very first things she saw when she turned on the light.

Pedro traveled with her everywhere. He remained a

loyal knight sworn to her service and dealt with all sorts of mundane things so that Celia wouldn't have to.

Celia and Pedro decided to celebrate their twenty-fifth wedding anniversary with a magnificent party—one they couldn't afford (and didn't want) at the time the two first married in a simple civil ceremony in 1962.

Invitations went out to every corner of the world. Celia deliberately put the wrong hour on those invitations to account for "Cuban Time" (a separate and unhurried time zone). She wanted to make sure that her fellow Cubans on the guest list would still arrive in a timely fashion.

Celia began the day of the party with her customary café cubano and the indulgence of a royal bath. Her friend and beautician Ruth Sanchez, who crafted La Reina's increasingly flamboyant style for the stage, worked her magic and sprinkled wildflowers in Celia's hair.

Mary, Zoila, and Brujita flew in from Miami to help with all the last-minute errands. The trio were Celia's dearest friends, the ones who picked her up at the airport and brought her to the Shrine of Our Lady of Charity in Coconut Grove every time Celia traveled to that capital of Cubanity in the United States. Now they made sure that everything went smoothly for the party. (Brujita earned the nickname "Little Witch" as a kid, when she liked to wear scarves and kerchiefs on her head. Cubans have a bit of a reputation for giving nicknames to everyone and everything.)

Family arrived. Celia's sister Gladys was there with her husband and three kids. Celia's brothers from the Sonora Matancera celebrated with her bandmates from the Fania All-Stars. Celia herself danced until her feet hurt. She danced as much as she had when she was fourteen years old and surrounded by her very first carnaval in Havana.

La Reina de Salsa received more honors and awards over the course of her long career than these few pages could possibly count. New York City gave her the Mayor's Award of Honor for Art and Culture alongside Nobel laureate Toni Morrison. Miami changed the name of Eighth Street in Little Havana to Celia Cruz Way. She also had an asteroid named after her.

The Grammy Awards couldn't stop nominating Celia; she wore a bright

blue wig to the ceremony on the night that she finally won her first of five Grammys. The Hollywood Walk of Fame dedicated a star to Celia Cruz after thousands of letters demanded it.

Here's how that Hollywood star happened: DJ Pepe Reyes took up some airtime to vent about Hollywood's indifference to Latin American entertainers, and he dropped Celia's name as a perfect example. Why didn't Celia Cruz have a Hollywood star *already*?

Journalist Winnie Sánchez was listening to the show, and it sparked her to start a campaign. She got in touch with Pepe Reyes. He spread the word by radio. His listeners sent letters on Celia's behalf to the Hollywood Chamber of Commerce, which selects the stars they consider worthy of inclusion.

The Chamber of Commerce was very confused and somewhat annoyed when those letters started pouring in. This wasn't how their star-selecting process usually worked. They got in touch with DJ Pepe's radio station to sheepishly ask, "Who is Celia Cruz?"

Avalanches of letters kept coming. The campaign spread to every Spanish-speaking station on the US airwaves. Many years after irate listeners wrote angry letters to Radio Progreso, hoping to get Celia fired from the Sonora Matancera, a new generation petitioned for her acknowledgment and praise.

The campaign worked. The Hollywood Walk of Fame added Celia's star to its constellation. The Chamber of Commerce reached out to Pepe Reyes to break the news on his radio show. Winnie Sánchez told Celia, who was sure that the whole thing was a hoax until the moment when she finally saw it in writing.

More praise and recognition followed. Yale University offered Celia an honorary doctorate for her contributions to music. During the graduation ceremony at Yale, she remembered another graduation in Havana, when her favorite teacher had urged Celia to follow her musical calling. The memory made Celia realize that she had honored both her father's wishes and her own; she had never stopped being a teacher. Celia taught music, and the whole world was her classroom. The audience of Yale graduates gave her a standing ovation when she received her diploma at the dais.

Less than a month later Celia joined her brothers-in-music for the Sonora Matancera orchestra's seventy-fifth anniversary concert. The whole audience jumped to their feet the instant that the music started, stayed on their feet throughout the whole show, and afterward roared applause for an entire five-minute ovation. (Five minutes might not sound like a long time, in which case I encourage you to set a timer and start clapping. Imagine yourself in a crowd of thousands. Pay attention to exactly how long it takes to reach the five-minute mark.)

One of Celia's strangest honors was the creation of a Barbie-size doll that sang tiny, tinny recordings of "Guantana-mera" and shouted "¡Azúcar!" The doll didn't sound much like Celia. The lighter shade of its plastic skin didn't look much like Celia, either. Despite those shortcomings she still supported the doll, because all profits went to her friend and stylist Ruth Sanchez and helped to pay medical bills for Ruth's son.

Every now and then a journalist would ask Celia what she thought of Fidel Castro. She told them all to go pester Fidel about what he thought of her instead.

¡GUANTANAMERA!

The wider world adored Celia Cruz as a musical queen, but her voice remained outlawed and silenced on the island of her birth. Cuba's most beloved cultural ambassador had been welcome everywhere but home.

After her mother died, Celia vowed to never set foot on Cuban soil for as long as Fidel Castro lived. She kept both the letter and the spirit of that vow, but she *also* took advantage of a fascinating loophole.

In 1990 Celia received an invitation to perform at the US naval base in Guantánamo—a small patch of American territory in southeastern Cuba, claimed by the US Navy since 1903. Today, Guantánamo—also called Gitmo—is most known for its role as a place for forced interrogations during the War on Terror following the September 11 terrorist attacks in 2001.

By visiting Guantánamo, Celia would be able to briefly revisit the *island* of Cuba while still remaining outside the *country* of Cuba.

She accepted the invitation.

Thirty years had passed since Celia and Pedro had flown out of Havana and into exile. Now the two of them climbed onto another plane and flew homeward, returning to a Cuba that was not the one they left.

GUANTÁNAMERA

The origin story of Cuba's most famous piece of music is a little bit fuzzy and often disputed; the musician Joseíto Fernández probably wrote the original love song about a country girl from Guantánamo in 1929. Something about that melody turned out to be an ideal foundation for newly improvised lyrics, so Fernández used the same tune to sing about current events on his radio show.

Next the composer Julián Orbón took that foundational tune and combined it with verses by José Martí, the national poet of Cuba. Martí died in battle fighting for Cuban independence from Spain, but lines from his *Versos sencillos* are often quoted—and sung—in the spirit of reconciliation, forgiveness, and peace:

Cultivo una rosa blanca,
en junio como en enero,
para el amigo sincero
que me da su mano franca.

Y para el cruel que me arranca
El corazón con que vivo,
Cardo ni ortiga cultivo;
Cultivo una rosa blanca.

The narrator grows white roses in summer and in winter. He offers them both to honest friends and to enemies who inflict heart-rending wounds.

Martí's verses remain the most famous and enduring lyrics to "Guantanamera," but the tune has also retained both its infinite adaptability *and* its paradoxical relationship to conflict: British soccer fans have been using it as a fight song to insult rival teams with new lyrics in English.

Celia added her own characteristic flourishes and improvisations whenever she sang "Guantanamera"—which was pretty much all the time. She sang it with the Fania All-Stars in the central African nation formerly known as Zaire. She sang it with movie star Antonio Banderas during an improvised, unscripted scene in the film *Mambo Kings*. She sang it with opera star Luciano Pavarotti at an AIDS benefit concert, and with hip-hop star Wyclef Jean on his album *The Carnival*.

Celia also sang "Guantanamera" at the Guantánamo naval base in 1990.

The plane ride took longer than Celia expected. They had to fly around the full length of the island to reach Guantánamo Bay in the southeast, because flying directly over the island and through Cuban airspace was forbidden to American aircraft. Celia felt a strange mix of sorrow and excitement while taking the long way around her island home.

The plane finally landed. Celia and Pedro disembarked together and took deep breaths of tropical air. They were home, and also further away from home than they had ever been.

Celia crossed the runway on foot. She walked right up to the fence that separated the rest of the island nation from that small patch of territory claimed by the US Navy. Somewhere on the other side of the fence lived friends and relatives Celia hadn't seen in three decades, young nieces and nephews she had never met.

She stuck her arm through the fence, grabbed a handful of Cuban soil from the minefield on the other side, and put it in a small bag for safekeeping. Then she gave the bag to Pedro. "Bury me with this." If Celia died before Fidel, she wanted to share a grave in New York City with that fistful of Cuban soil. (If Fidel died first, then she wanted to come home and claim a gravesite next to Ollita.)

Onstage at the naval base Celia sang the music of the

island back to the island. She gave "Guantanamera" back to Guantánamo Bay. Royal palm trees swayed as though dancing to her performance of "Canto a La Habana," a song of praise that names several beautiful places in Cuba and still insists that "la Habana no admite comparación." Nothing will ever compare to Havana, Celia's hometown, still bustling on the other side of the island and the other side of that heavily guarded fence.

She broke down sobbing before she could finish the song.

The stage was usually her sanctuary, a source of power

that she had always used to sing her way through raw grief and overwhelming pain, but to be so close and so far away from home was more than even Cella's voice could hold all at once.

The band played on. The music held her up. Celia pulled herself together, sang the last lines—"ay Cuba, ay Cuba, tus paisajes"—and then cried out, "¡Azúcar!" She knew how to savor both the bitter and the sweet.

No roses of reconciliation ever grew between Fidel Castro and Celia Cruz, and after that day she never returned to the island.

In 1994 Celia was asked to perform at another military base, this time in Panama. Tens of thousands of Cuban refugees who fled on makeshift rafts were being plucked from the waves before they could reach Florida and detained at US Navy bases throughout the Caribbean.

Celia agreed to sing for the balseros (rafters) held in Panama, and she was appalled by the conditions she found in the detainment center. Her fellow Cuban refugees had been fenced in like animals—including the children and newborns among them. Such inhumane treatment was something Celia expected from the Castro regime but not from the government of her adopted home. At Guantánamo she had performed through her sorrow; in Panama she sang through her rage.

Most of the refugees were too young to remember a time before the revolution, when it was legal in Cuba to play records by Celia Cruz, but to her great surprise they all knew who she was. The balseros knew her music and sang along. Fidel Castro had done everything he could to obliterate her from Cuba's collective memory and musical history, and he had failed.

One of the refugees made a tiny model of a raft and passed it through the audience. Every hand held it up like a sea wave. The raft made its way to safety, to Celia herself. She brought it back to the States, where she fought hard for the rafters by petitioning President Bill Clinton directly—something that La Reina could easily do, because the president had just awarded her the National Medal of Arts. Most of the balseros were soon able to follow that tiny raft and immigrate to the United States.

Celia was an elder now. Her Majesty laughed at any suggestion that she should maybe slow down, and continued to tour worldwide. She joked about dying onstage with the echoing taste of one final ¡Azúcar! on her smiling lips.

Her enthusiasm for new collaborations, musical possibilities, and overlapping genres continued to grow. She recorded with David Byrne after her nephew shared a *Talking Heads* album, joined Wyclef Jean for their aforementioned (and Grammy-nominated) "Guantanamera," and joyfully kept pace with Puerto Rican reggaeton artist Mikey Perfecto in the (also Grammy-nominated) song "La negra tiene tumbao." She often quoted the old Spanish proverb "Él que no cambia se estanca." (Those who cannot change will stagnate instead.)

Before Celia's annual checkup in 2002 she had no reason to suspect that she had any health problems whatsoever. The Caribbean girl never even caught a cold, despite weathering so many snowy winters in New York City.

She was shocked when a mammogram discovered the beginnings of a breast tumor.

Celia's cancer diagnosis was terrifying all by itself. It also carried new waves of old grief; the same disease had claimed Ollita. This time she couldn't find sanctuary onstage. Exhausted by the cancer treatments, Celia left her touring life behind—though of course she didn't stop performing *entirely*, and still took the stage at the Grammy

Awards after earning no fewer than four additional nominations.

Her doctors scheduled a mastectomy. She scheduled a magazine interview and photo shoot for the night before. "Make me look as nice as possible," Celia whispered to Ruth while getting her makeup ready for the shoot. "They're going to remove my breast early tomorrow morning. These will be the last pictures taken with my bust intact."

Surgery was successful. The doctors told Celia that she was cured. She celebrated her fortieth wedding anniversary with Pedro by taking an actual vacation in France and Italy, which the two of them considered their long-overdue honeymoon.

Cancer wasn't finished with Celia yet, however. The first and most frightening hint that something was still horribly wrong happened later that year, and it happened onstage.

She was back in Mexico City, performing for a tribute concert held in her honor. An entire half century had passed since she had lived here, newly exiled from Cuba and newly in love with her trumpet-playing knight. Now Pedro joined her onstage to sing a surprise duet.

First she felt overjoyed to share the moment with him.

Then she forgot the lyrics of the song.

That *never* happened.

Celia knew every line of every song in her repertoire. She knew them backward, forward, and inside out. She knew the lyrics well enough to spontaneously rewrite them and to improvise new vocal flourishes around them. Every word had been chiseled into the foundation stones of Celia's whole being. Those lyrics had never abandoned her before.

No one else really noticed—not even Pedro. The duet was already a spontaneous moment that they hadn't rehearsed, and it came at the very end of the concert. Thunderous applause followed immediately after Celia's lapse of memory. La Reina graciously thanked her audience. Then she left the stage, left Mexico City, and made another doctor's appointment as soon as she got back to New York.

This time they found a cancerous tumor in her brain.

She underwent another tumor-removing surgery in December 2002. Afterward her biggest complaint was that a hospital employee tried to cover for her by telling the press that she had come in for plastic surgery. Celia was incensed. The whole idea that she would want to change anything about her smile or the proud Blackness of her features made her angry enough to contradict the news story by publicly disclosing her medical condition.

She asked the media for respect and privacy.

She visited with friends and family.

She also got back to work, recording what would become her final album.

No one knows exactly how many records Celia cut over the long course of her extraordinary career. It depends who you ask. Many of the original albums were destroyed along with any evidence that they had ever existed at all, the vinyl melted down to be recast as someone else's music. Regardless of which number historians accept as accurate, *Regalo del Alma* was her eightieth album at least. The title echoes José Martí lines of verse, which Celia sang a thousand times in "Guantanamera": "y antes de morirme quiero / echar mis versos del alma" ("and before dying / I want to throw the verses of my soul"). She sang the gift of her soul into that final album, recorded over the course of ten days in early 2003.

Her brain tumor returned and grew larger.

Pedro continued to bring fresh-brewed café cubano to Celia's bedside every morning, the tray decorated with a small yellow flower.

Her brother, Bárbaro, died in Havana. No one told Celia. She was already slipping in and out of consciousness, and during her lucid moments Pedro couldn't bear to give her the news. She never found out about missing another family funeral.

Celia heard the first cuts of *Regalo del Alma* that summer from her hospital bed. She could no longer speak, but she seemed to approve. Her fingers tapped along with the beat.

La Reina died of cancer in the afternoon of July 16, 2003, at the age of seventy-seven.

CHAPTER SEVEN

HER LEGACY

Take a moment to remember when a song became the soundtrack of your life. Maybe you heard it performed live onstage, or alone through headphones. Maybe you heard those lyrics in the rapid movements of a sign interpreter. However it happened, try to conjure up that same moment now. Remember when a piece of music seemed to belong to you and only you.

For a vast and immeasurable number of souls, that moment of hearing their own personal soundtrack was performed by Celia Cruz. She sang like your favorite tía. She also sang like a goddess remaking the world.

Within hours of Celia's death, the word *¡Azúcar!* appeared in fresh graffiti all over Havana. The Cuban government issued a command that every ¡Azúcar! must be painted over immediately. They kept trying to erase Celia Cruz from her hometown, over and over again, and they continued to fail. More posthumous tags of ¡Azúcar! showed up on walls everywhere.

The city of Havana mourned a daughter.

The people of Havana mourned a queen.

Her body traveled by motorcade from the New Jersey house she bought with Pedro to a funeral home in Manhattan, first crossing the George Washington Bridge and passing through Washington Heights. Crowds gathered in the street of the Latino neighborhood. People held flowers, held each other, and reached out to touch the hearse as it rolled slowly by.

Ruth Sanchez was already waiting at the funeral home, ready to work her magic on Celia's hair and makeup one final time. "She died without knowing how great she was," Ruth said. "Celia had her feet on the ground."

From there the casket traveled by plane to Miami, the capital city of Cubanity in exile, where Celia lay in state at the Freedom Tower on Biscayne Boulevard.

Hundreds of thousands of mourners surrounded the tower. They did not mourn silently. Music played. People danced, sang, chanted her name, and cried out "¡Azúcar!" in celebration of Celia's fierce joy and her limitless ability to savor both the bitter and the sweet.

Miami's Metrorail ran for free that day. None of the mourners needed to scrounge for pocket change to pay the fare the way that Celia and her friends had when they took the bus to see their first carnaval.

Her body returned to New York City for the funeral ceremony, held on July 22, 2003. It rained hard. Hundreds of thousands of mourners flocked to Manhattan, got soaked in the rain, and shouted "¡Azúcar!" at the thundering sky.

Pedro Knight carefully placed the fistful of Cuban soil in Celia's casket, as she had requested of him. "Of all her fans," he said, "I'm surely the luckiest."

Patti LaBelle sang "Ave Maria" during the ceremony, and Victor Manuelle led an a cappella adaptation of "La vida es un carnaval."

A horse-drawn carriage bore Celia away from Saint

Patrick's Cathedral, her casket wrapped in the Cuban flag. Sunlight broke through the rain clouds, right on cue. Many thousands of voices held up her name, sang in the streets, and offered La Reina her last standing ovation.

July 16—the day that Celia died—is also the birthday of the great Panamanian salsero Rubén Blades. He had this to say about his colleague:

> Celia Cruz could take any song and make it unforgettable. She transcended matter. With Celia, even the simplest of songs got infused with her vigor and personality. I don't think one can listen to anything she did and be indifferent. With her powerful voice and her spectacular presentations, she helped take the world of salsa to an international level, and her legacy will live forever. Real death occurs when one forgets, but we are not going to forget Celia ever.

Celia herself said this on the same topic: "When someone asks me how I want to be remembered, I always say

the same thing: I want everybody to think of me as someone who was full of joy."

Her legacy as a music teacher with a planet-size classroom lives on in the Celia Cruz Bronx High School of
Music, founded in 2003. Her love of teaching also inspired
the creation of the Celia Cruz Foundation, which offers
scholarships to young Latinx students of music.

She remembered what it was like to pay for textbooks
with money that she earned singing radio jingles. She also
remembered studying at the Havana music academy under the cold ire of her father's disapproval.

Celia knew that the past and the future would always
need to keep in touch, so she did everything she could
think of to uplift new generations of musicians. She was a
force of community who made far-flung pockets of Latinidad visible to one another, and she left behind lessons of
kinship and joy as a means of survival.

Listen to one of those lessons now. Go find a copy of her final
album, *Regalo del Alma*. The front cover shows Celia grinning
in a huge silver wig. The first track is "Ella tiene fuego," another

rap collaboration, this time with the Panamanian founding father of reggaeton, El General. The last track is "Yo viviré," an adaptation of Gloria Gaynor's "I Will Survive" that transforms the iconic breakup song into a mini biography of Celia Cruz.

Play it.

The first two words are *mi voz* ("my voice"). Pay attention to the vocal precision of her rare contralto, the way that she snaps every syllable and savors those extra, rolling *R*s added to the rhyming ends of *volar* ("fly") and *atravesar* ("pass through").

She goes on to sing about crossing borders and breaking down barriers. She sings about memories and friends left behind. She sings about the comparsa troupes of carnaval that she first saw at fourteen. She sings about rumba, son, and guaracha, traditions of Afro-Cuban music born on the eastern side of the island and mastered by the Sonora Matancera. She sings about resilience in diaspora and exile, and she does so in Spanish.

Many producers tried to convince Celia to sing in English over the years. They were sure that this was the only possible way to become a star in the United States, and they wanted her music to reach as many people as possible. Such well-meaning producers could not imagine an America that would listen to Celia Cruz if she continued to sing in Spanish.

Celia resisted this immense pressure to translate herself. She sang in the language of her heart, and America listened. The musical culture of the United States would never be the same.

The lyrics of "Yo viviré" pun on claves, the percussion instruments that Celia used to keep time when she won her first singing contest—a word that also means "code" or "key." She reminds us that the past can help unlock the future, and she offers sugar as a gift instead of a welcoming shout: "mi azúcar para ti." Accept that gift. Someday you might need it.

Survivors of the 2016 Pulse tragedy in Orlando, Florida, shared the word *azúcar* with one another as a mantra, and adopted "Yo viviré" as an anthem of endurance in a time of overwhelming grief. Celia is still a force of community.

Play the song again. Sing the last line along with her:

"Yo viviré, yo viviré, yo viviré, y sobreviviré."

I will survive.

Celia conquered the world with her voice and her huge heart," said the Cuban-born singer Lucrecia, who played La Reina in the most recent of three different musicals based on the life story of Celia Cruz. "She was noble, a woman of the old school. She remembered everyone's name. You'd meet her once and she'd be sending you postcards for the rest of her life."

Lucrecia grew up in Celia's old neighborhood of Santos Suárez, trained at the Instituto Superior de Arte de Cuba, and heard Celia's voice for the first time on a contraband record of the Sonora Matancera. She settled in Spain, unable to return to Cuba after criticizing the government in song, and performed with Celia in 1998.

Some critics have praised Lucrecia as Celia's heir—the queen is dead, long live the queen—but Lucrecia does her best to squelch those comparisons: "I can't, even for a moment, consider the possibility of being her successor. Nobody can be. She was the goddess of Cuban music. She still is."

Unlike her late friend and mentor, Lucrecia doesn't feel the same longing or nostalgia for her lost island home. "But not wanting to go back there doesn't make me less Cuban," she insists. "Cuban is what I am, period."

Él que no cambia se estanca.

Those who cannot change will stagnate instead.

Celia's legacy and influence on Broadway musicals extends beyond those three aforementioned theatrical biographies. She wasn't the only New York City musician brainstorming new ways to mix salsa and hip-hop at the turn of the century, when Lin-Manuel Miranda of *Hamilton* fame wrote the earliest versions of *In the Heights*.

Miranda's first Broadway hit begins with claves. "The clave beat is the DNA sequence of a lot of Latin rhythms," said Quiara Alegría Hudes, coauthor of the play and screenplay. Celia began her career with claves in hand, channeling her favorite singer to win her first radio contest. She also ended her last album with "Yo viviré," which praises claves as the keys to every generation.

The very first bit of dialogue in *Heights* is shared between Usnavi (the narrator/protagonist) and Piragua Guy, an otherwise unnamed pregonero who belts out a street vendor's cry—a Puerto Rican pregón—thereby briefly becoming the voice of a city. The pregón is also in the DNA of Latin music and verse. Margarita Engle honored an ice cream–peddling pregonero in her verse memoir. Beny Moré was the street-level voice of Havana at seventeen as a pregonero singing about fruit. Celia Cruz sang traditional pregónes like "El pregón del pescador" in the early days of her radio stardom, and again in the early days of salsa.

Miranda put together a playlist of salsa ancestry in 2017

called "I relish your wit! I SALSA YOUR FACE," and of course it includes Celia Cruz. "If you don't feel the need to move to this, notify your next of kin," he said of "Químbara." "Celia is the greatest."

The movie version of *In the Heights* further acknowledges its ancestral debt to Celia Cruz as one of several graffiti murals commemorating Latina matriarchs. (Celia shows up right between Frida Kahlo and Dolores Huerta.) Iris, the young character in the film who represents the promise of the future, has that whole list of founding mothers memorized.

The past and the future will always need to keep in touch.

None of us knows what the next chapter of Cuban history and music will bring. We do, however, know how the power struggle between Fidel Castro and Celia Cruz finally ended.

El Comandante outlived La Guarachera by thirteen years—which does not mean that he won. He retired from the Cuban government in 2011. Celia was cleared from the official list of banned musicians almost immediately afterward, in 2012.

The Voice of Cuba returned to the airwaves of her island home.

DID YOU KNOW?

★ Celia's full name was Úrsula Hilaria Celia Caridad Cruz Alfonso.

★ In addition to receiving the National Medal of Arts, Celia Cruz also added the title of doctor to her lengthy list of achievements. She was honored with three different doctorates: an honorary doctoral degree of music from Yale in 1989; an honorary doctorate from Florida International University in 1992; and an honorary doctorate in music from the University of Miami in 1999.

celiacruzfoundation.com/celiacruzbiography

★ In 2006, the Smithsonian National Museum of American History featured Celia Cruz with a special exhibition: "¡Azúcar! The Life and Music of Celia Cruz." In 2012, Celia was also honored in one of the museum's Artifact Walls, where artist Robert Weingarten created a "visual biography" of Celia after a public vote on which of five historical figures should be the subject of the new portrait. The exhibition looked at Celia's colorful appearance and recognition during her career. This included wigs, shoes from her collection, one of her five Grammys, and more.

si.edu/newsdesk/releases/national-museum-american
-history-reveals-celia-cruz-portrait

★ Considered "the Queen of Latin Music" and having dominated the Latin music scene for almost fifty years, Celia recorded at least eighty albums, received over one hundred awards, and appeared in ten movies. Of those albums, twenty went gold and eight went platinum.

atom.library.miami.edu/chc5070

★ "If I have to belittle myself to make money, I'd rather not have any" was Celia's response after not getting paid for a performance for refusing to sing one of Fidel Castro's favorite songs, "Burundanga."

youtube.com/watch?v=c5NbB-M4NZk

★ In 2015, Telemundo released *Celia*, a telenovela based

on La Reina de Salsa's life. The following year "La negra tiene tumbao" won Television Theme Song of the Year at the American Society of Composers, Authors and Publishers Awards.

telemundo.com/shows/celia

★ In 2011, the United States Postal Service celebrated the Afro-Cuban singer by including her image in their Latin Music Legends US postage stamp series.

postalmuseum.si.edu/stamp-stories-celia-cruz

A NOTE FROM WILLIAM ALEXANDER

Right now, as I type these words in the summer of 2021, new waves of protests against the autocratic Cuban government are spreading across the island to a degree unseen since 1959. People in the streets are chanting "patria y vida" (homeland and life), an inversion and rebuke of Fidel Castro's favorite slogan: "patria o muerte" (homeland or death)—a nationalistic demand to sacrifice everything for Castro's revolution.

The new protest slogan comes from a rap song written in solidarity with the San Isidro Movement of artists and journalists who demonstrate against government repression. Yotuel Romero, one of the many cowriters of "Patria y vida," is best known as a member of the Orishas—Afro-Cuban expats who started to mix hip-hop with traditional Cuban rhythms at the turn of the century, just like Celia before them.

History is always happening; so is the art and music that we need to understand it.

A NOTE FROM HISPANIC STAR

When Hispanic Star decided to join Macmillan and Roaring Brook Press in creating this chapter book biography series, our intention was to share stories of incredible Hispanic leaders with young readers, inspiring them through the acts of those Stars.

For centuries, the Hispanic community has made significant contributions to different spaces of our collective culture and everyday life—whether it's sports, entertainment, art, politics, or business—and we wanted to showcase some of the role models who made this possible. We especially wanted to inspire Hispanic children to rise up and take the mantle of Hispanic unity and pride.

With Hispanic Star, we also wanted to shine a light on the common language that unifies a large portion of the Latinx community. *Hispanic* means "Spanish speaking" and frequently refers to people whose origins are from a country where Spanish is the primary language spoken. The term *Latinx*, in all its deviations, is broader and more inclusive, referring to people of all gender identities from all countries in Latin America and their descendants, many of whom were born in the United States.

This groundbreaking chapter book series can be found in both English and Spanish, as a tribute to the Hispanic community in our country.

We encourage all our readers to get to know these heroes and the positive impact they continue to have, inviting future generations to learn more about the different journeys of our unique and charming Hispanic Stars!